W9-AQF-049

P I R A T E S

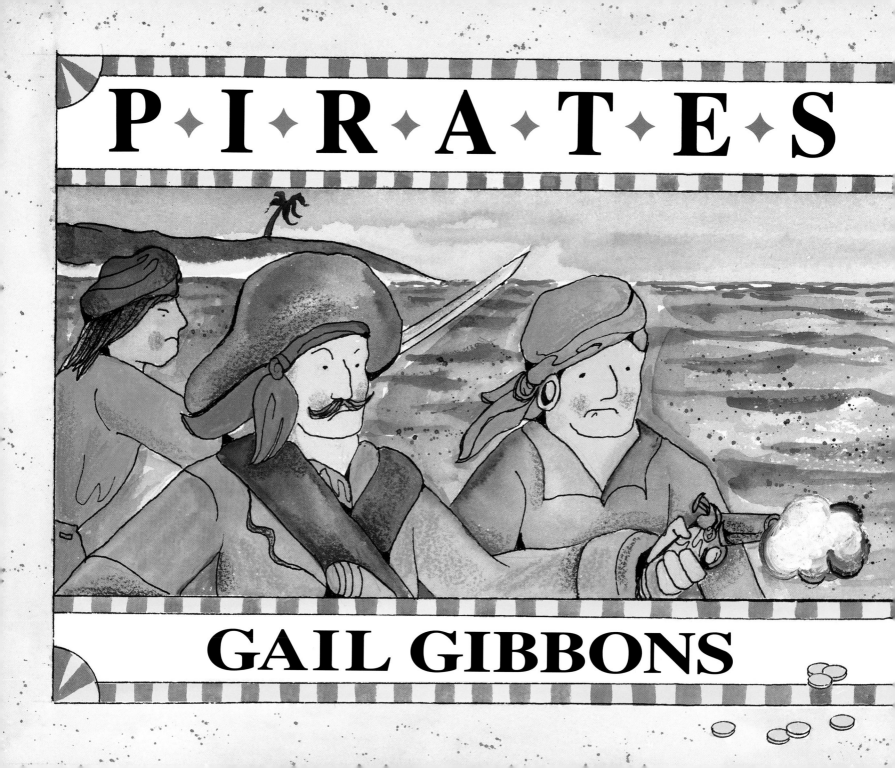

GAIL GIBBONS

Robbers of the High Seas

Little, Brown and Company

BOSTON   NEW YORK   LONDON

J 910.45 G3526p 1993
Gibbons, Gail.
Pirates   NOV 09 '11

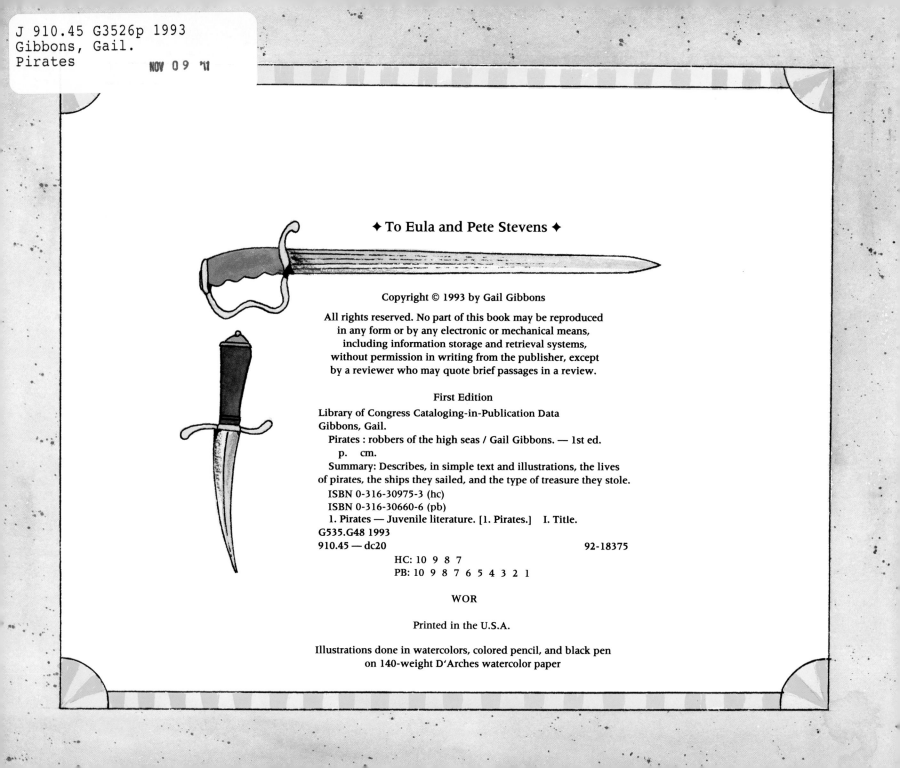

♦ **To Eula and Pete Stevens** ♦

Copyright © 1993 by Gail Gibbons

All rights reserved. No part of this book may be reproduced
in any form or by any electronic or mechanical means,
including information storage and retrieval systems,
without permission in writing from the publisher, except
by a reviewer who may quote brief passages in a review.

First Edition

Library of Congress Cataloging-in-Publication Data
Gibbons, Gail.
  Pirates : robbers of the high seas / Gail Gibbons. — 1st ed.
    p.   cm.
  Summary: Describes, in simple text and illustrations, the lives
of pirates, the ships they sailed, and the type of treasure they stole.
  ISBN 0-316-30975-3 (hc)
  ISBN 0-316-30660-6 (pb)
  1. Pirates — Juvenile literature. [1. Pirates.]   I. Title.
G535.G48 1993
910.45 — dc20   92-18375
              HC: 10 9 8 7
              PB: 10 9 8 7 6 5 4 3 2 1

                        WOR

              Printed in the U.S.A.

Illustrations done in watercolors, colored pencil, and black pen
        on 140-weight D'Arches watercolor paper

Pirates are robbers of the high seas. They began to roam the seas as soon as people set sail to travel the oceans and explore new worlds. Stories about pirates and how they lived come from old diaries, letters, and ships' logs.

Thousands of years ago, the Greeks and Romans ran the risk of having their ships taken over by pirates. Pirates even kidnapped their people. Once they kidnapped a famous Roman leader, Julius Caesar, and held him prisoner until the ransom was paid.

These pirates were very powerful. They banded together to attack the trading ships in order to steal their cargo.

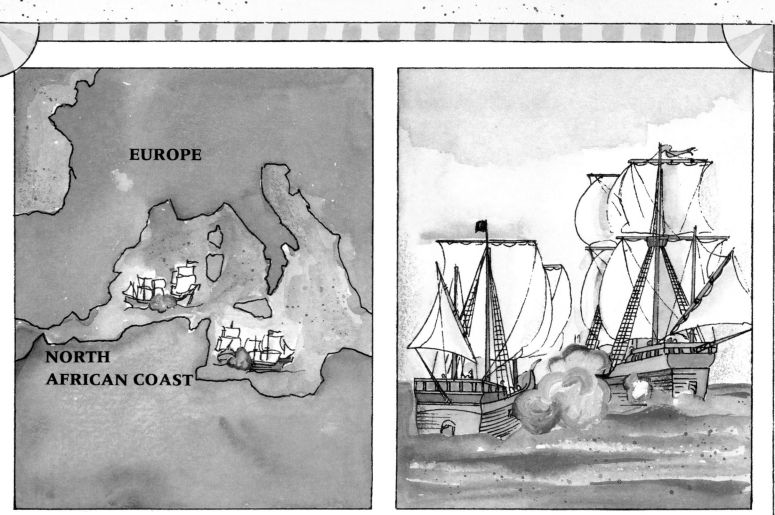

EUROPE

NORTH
AFRICAN COAST

Around 1300, bands of ruthless pirates set up settlements along the North African coast. For many years they attacked and looted ships that sailed off the coast of their settlement, the Barbary States. These people were known as the famous Barbary pirates.

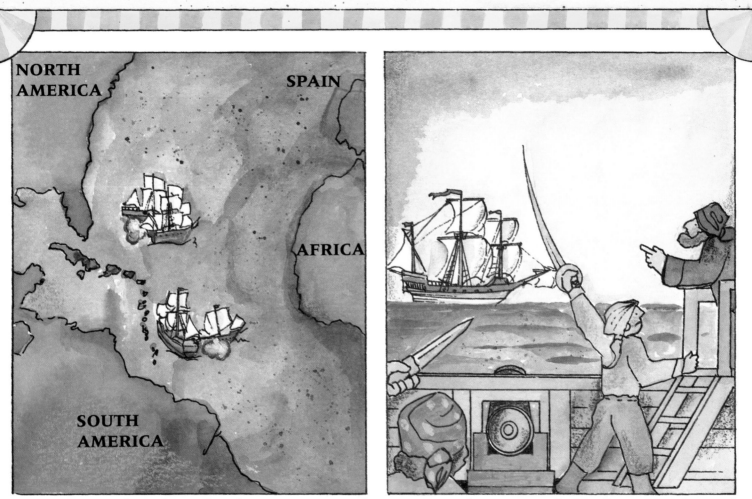

About five hundred years ago, when Spain discovered the fine goods and treasures of the New World, pirates became a special danger. The news of Spanish treasure ships carrying emeralds, gold, silver, pearls, and other cargo back to Europe spread among the pirates.

The Spanish traders sailed large armed ships called galleons. The pirates watched for the returning galleons, especially those coming from the major trading ports of Havana, Cartagena, and Porto Bello.

No treasure ship was safe from the fierce and greedy pirates. They wanted the treasure for themselves.

The pirates' ships were smaller and faster than the galleons. They could be easily maneuvered through the high seas.

Pirate ships were also well armed. When the pirates began to attack, they fired heavy cannons. The cannonballs shot holes through the galleons' billowing sails.

The galleons' sailors carried weapons for their protection. They fired at the pirate ships to stop them from attacking.

But the cannonballs shot from the pirates' cannons often wrecked the galleons. With sails flapping, splintered masts, broken decks, and other damage, the treasure ships were unable to escape the vicious pirates.

The pirates sailed their ships close enough to the galleons to jump on board. Daggers flashed. Swords waved. Pistols fired. The treasure ships' crews tried to defend their valuable cargo.

Sometimes the galleon captains and their crews battled until they won. But many times the pirates won. Then they robbed the ships of their treasure. According to legend, pirates would make the captain and crew walk the plank.

Before shoving off, pirates often set fire to the plundered galleons. All traces of their evil doings burned and sank to the bottom of the sea.

Then the pirates divvied up the treasure among themselves. Often the loot was too heavy to carry around, and the pirates quickly spent it or sold the riches at seaport towns.

Other pirates buried their treasure in secret places. They drew maps so they'd be able to find their bounty later.

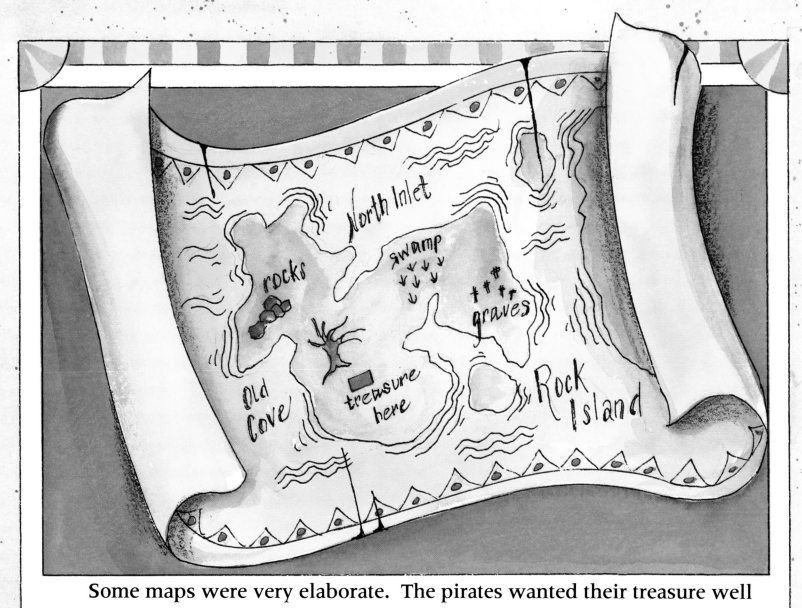

Some maps were very elaborate. The pirates wanted their treasure well hidden!

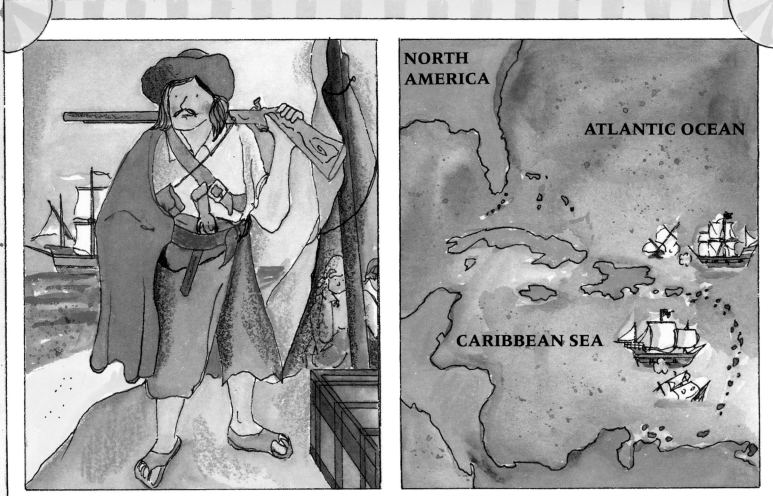

Around 1600, there were other pirates called buccaneers. The buccaneers were made up of English, Dutch, and French settlers living on the Caribbean islands. Spain claimed it owned some of these lands and didn't want the buccaneers living there.

The buccaneers banded together to protect themselves from Spain.
Soon they began pirating Spanish ports and treasure ships. They challenged
Spain's power in the Caribbean.

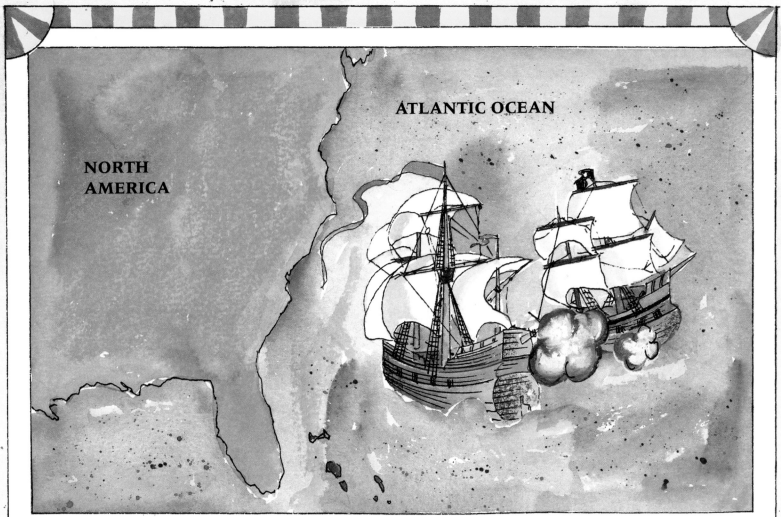

During the 1700s, most pirates robbed ships in the Atlantic Ocean. They attacked and stole goods being shipped along the coast of North America.

The pirates were loyal to no country. They sailed their ships under their own frightening flags, raising them when they were ready to attack. Often they flew a skull-and-crossbones flag, the Jolly Roger. Some people think the name Jolly Roger came from *joli rouge*, "pretty red" in French. Others think it came from Old Roger, an English name for the devil.

Pirates were outlaws of the sea. Often they were hunted down. When they were captured, they were put on trial. Those pirates found guilty were usually sentenced to be hanged.

But not all pirates were bad. Some were hired by kings and queens of great countries to rob the ships of their enemies. These pirates were called privateers and were considered heroes.

Eventually there were fewer and fewer pirates. More were conquered in sea battles; more were captured. Hundreds of years have passed since the mighty pirates ruled the seas. Nowadays, most of the oceans and seas are safe for travel. The Jolly Roger no longer flies.

Some buried treasure remains lost forever. The life of a pirate was dangerous, and some pirates did not live long enough to return to claim the treasure they had hidden away. Today, treasure hunters still search for the long-hidden treasures of the pirates.

FAMOUS PIRATES

SIR HENRY MORGAN was a Welsh buccaneer. He attacked Spanish and Dutch settlements in the Caribbean. In 1671, he defeated Panama City with a force of two thousand men and added more riches to his coffers.

EDWARD TEACH, also called Blackbeard, was a mean, blood-thirsty English pirate. In 1717, he captured a large French vessel, renamed it *Queen Anne's Revenge,* and used it as his own pirate ship. He and his crew stalked their prey in the Caribbean and along the coast of Virginia and the Carolinas.

CAPTAIN KIDD was commissioned to capture pirates off the East African coast by King William of England in 1695. Instead, because of pressure from his crew and his own greed, he turned traitor and became a pirate himself. He was captured and hanged in 1701.

ANNE BONNEY was one of the few women pirates. In the early 1700s, she fell in love with the pirate Calico Jack Rackham and joined him and his crew.

MARY READ was another famous woman pirate. Disguised as a man, she served aboard the same ship as Anne Bonney.

JOHN AVERY was an English pirate in the late 1600s. As captain of the *Fancy,* he preyed on ships in the Red Sea, including British traders and the treasure-laden vessels of India's ruler, the Great Mogul. His adventures were exaggerated and retold in songs, a novel, and a play, making him a famous swashbuckling figure even in his own lifetime. Eventually, however, on the run from the law, he returned to England, lost all his money in a foolish business decision, and died poor.

BARTHOLOMEW ROBERTS, better known as Black Bart, captured and plundered more than four hundred ships in the early 1700s. He and his crew attacked ships from the Caribbean to Newfoundland to Africa.

CAPTAIN HOOK was a fictional pirate from the book *Peter Pan.* One of Captain Hook's hands was bitten off by a crocodile while he was fighting against Peter Pan and the Lost Boys. Captain Hook blamed Peter for the accident and vowed to get revenge.

YO, HO, HO!

Treasure hunters are still searching for the gold, silver, and other riches buried in secret places by pirates. Some treasures have remained hidden for over two hundred years!

✦ Blackbeard supposedly hid a huge cache of gold and silver near Ocracoke Inlet in North Carolina in the early 1700s. Every year more treasure hunters try to find where this booty is buried, but they still haven't uncovered it.

✦ Many expeditions have searched on Cocos Island, off the coast of Costa Rica, for a treasure called the Lost Loot of Lima. This treasure is said to have been hidden by the pirate Benito Bonito of the Bloody Sword and is estimated to be worth sixty-five million dollars!

✦ Since 1795, treasure hunters have been trying to dig to the bottom of a deep shaft on Oak Island off the coast of Nova Scotia. They believe pirates hid a huge bounty there in a network of connecting shafts and tunnels. But whenever they get close to the bottom, the shaft fills up with seawater — and they have to start all over again!

✦ Other pirate treasures are said to be buried along the Gulf Coast from Texas to Florida.

Happy Treasure Hunting!